THE
Prayers
OF JESUS
PARTICIPANT'S GUIDE

D0974243

The Deeper Connections Series

The Miracles of Jesus

The Parables of Jesus

The Prayers of Jesus

Deeper CONNECTIONS

THE

Prayers
OF JESUS

PARTICIPANT'S GUIDE

Six In-depth Studies Connecting the Bible to Life

Matt Williams
General Editor

ZONDERVAN®

ZONDERVAN.com/
AUTHORTRACKER
follow your favorite authors

We want to hear from you. Please send your comments about this book to us in care of zreview@zondervan.com. Thank you.

The Prayers of Jesus Participant's Guide
Copyright © 2007 by Matt Williams

Requests for information should be addressed to:

Zondervan, *Grand Rapids, Michigan 49530*

ISBN-10: 0-310-27197-5
ISBN-13: 978-0-310-27197-0

Interior design by Mark Sheeres

Printed in the United States of America

09 10 11 12 13 • 10 9 8 7

Contents

Preface

We all know Christians who are bored with Bible study — not because the Bible is boring, but because they haven't been introduced to its meaning in its first-century context and how that is significant for our lives today. When we begin to understand some of these "deeper connections" — both to the first century and to the twenty-first century — our lives are transformed.

The idea for the Deeper Connections series grew out of a concern that far too many Bible studies lack depth and solid biblical application. We wanted a Bible study series that was written and taught by biblical experts who could also communicate that material in a *clear, practical, understandable* manner. The Deeper Connections teachers have one foot in the historical, biblical text and the other in the modern world; they not only have written numerous books, they have many years of pastoral experience. When they teach in the local church, they often hear comments such as, "Wow, I've never heard it explained that way before." Unfortunately that's because, until recently, Bible professors usually spent most of their time writing books for other professors or occasionally for pastors, and the layperson in the church had little access to this biblical knowledge. Deeper Connections seeks to remedy this by bringing the best in biblical scholarship directly to small groups and Sunday school classes through the popular medium of DVD.

Don't be scared by the word "deeper" — deeper does not mean that these studies are hard to understand. It simply means that we are attempting to get at the true meaning of the biblical text, which involves investigating the historical, religious, and social background of first-century Jewish culture and their Greek and Roman neighbors. If we fail to study and understand this background, then we also fail to understand the deeper and true meaning of the Bible.

After making deeper connections to the biblical texts, the teachers then apply that text to life in the twenty-first century. This is where a deeper look into the text really pays off. Life-application in the church today has sometimes been a bit shallow and many times unrelated to the biblical passage itself. In this series, the practical application derives directly out of the biblical text.

So, to borrow the alternate title of *The Hobbit*, J. R. R. Tolkien's bestselling classic, we invite you to join us on an adventure to "there and back again"! Your life won't be the same as a result.

About the Video Teachers

Dr. Gary Burge is professor of New Testament at Wheaton College in Wheaton, Illinois, and a sought-after conference speaker. His experiences in Beirut, Lebanon, in the early 1970s when civil war broke out have helped him to see how valuable it is to understand the world of the Middle East in order to correctly understand the biblical world of Jesus. Gary is the author of many books, including a commentary on the gospel of John.

Dr. David Garland is professor of Christian Scriptures at Truett Theological Seminary, Baylor University, Waco, Texas. David is closely connected to local church ministry and has served as interim pastor of fifteen churches in Kentucky, Indiana, and Texas. He is the author of many books, including commentaries on the gospels of Matthew and Mark.

Dr. Mark Strauss is professor of New Testament at Bethel Seminary in San Diego, California. He is a frequent preacher at San Diego area churches and has served in three interim pastorates. Mark is the author of many books, including a commentary on the gospel of Luke and *Four Portraits, One Jesus: An Introduction to Jesus and the Gospels*.

Dr. Michael Wilkins is professor of New Testament Language and Literature and the dean of the faculty at Talbot School of Theology, Biola University, La Mirada, California. Michael speaks throughout the world about his two passions: surfing and discipleship. He was senior pastor of two different churches in California and has written numerous books, including two commentaries on the gospel of Matthew.

Dr. Matt Williams is associate professor of New Testament at Talbot School of Theology, Biola University, La Mirada, California. A former missionary to Spain, Matt preaches and teaches at churches throughout the United States and Spain. He is general editor of *Colección Teológica Contemporánea*, a series of theological books in Spanish, and is the author of two books on the Gospels.

Dr. Ben Witherington III is professor of New Testament at Asbury Theological Seminary in Wilmore, Kentucky. Ben is an avid fan of jazz and sports, especially the Atlanta Braves. He has led numerous study tours through the lands of the Bible and is known for bringing the text to life through incisive historical and cultural analysis. He is a prolific author, including commentaries on all four gospels.

Host **Jarrett Stevens** is director of the college and singles ministry and teacher for 7/22 at North Point Church in Alpharetta, Georgia. Prior to that he was on staff at Willow Creek Community Church in suburban Chicago.

Watch and Pray

Jesus' Model Prayer Life
(Mark 1:32–39; 9:9–29; 14:32–42)

Dr. David Garland

Very early in the morning, while it was still dark, Jesus got up, left the house and went off to a solitary place, where he prayed.

Mark 1:35

The essence of all prayer is that it is a conversation with God as the partner.

Oscar Cullmann

INTRODUCTION

Video Opener

Scripture Reading: Mark 1:32–39; 9:9–29; 14:32–42, followed by a prayer that God will open your heart as you study his Word

Location of Prayers: Capernaum, close to the Sea of Galilee; Mount of Transfiguration: perhaps Mount Hermon (near Caesarea Philippi, twenty-five miles north of the Sea of Galilee, cf. Mark 8:27); Garden of Gethsemane, Mount of Olives, Jerusalem

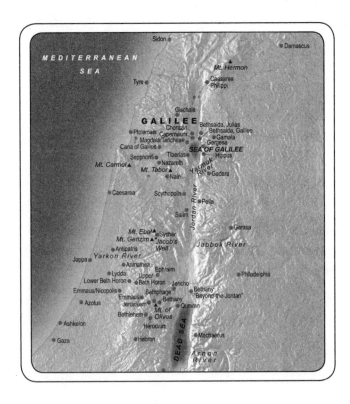

Faith & Trust in God.

CONNECTING TO THE BIBLE

Jesus' example shows us that it takes a lifestyle of prayer to face what lies before us.

Video Teaching #1 Notes

Location of Video Teaching: Colorado Rockies

Mark 1:32–39: first example of Jesus praying in Mark

Very early in the morning, while it was still dark, Jesus got up, left the house and went off to a solitary place, where he prayed.

Mark 1:35

But Jesus often withdrew to lonely places and prayed.

Luke 5:16

The disciples do not understand Jesus' need to pray

Simon and his companions went to look for him.

Mark 1:36

Amid spiritual victory, Jesus prays to keep himself centered on his mission

Jesus replied, "Let us go somewhere else — to the nearby villages — so I can preach there also. That is why I have come."

Mark 1:38

"Come away to a deserted place all by yourselves and rest a while."

Mark 6:31, NRSV

I must go away and take time for prayer and solitude.

Charles Spurgeon

Mark 9:9–29: second example of Jesus praying in Mark

The transfiguration on top of the mountain

He took Peter, John and James with him and went up onto a mountain to pray. *As he was praying*, the appearance of his face changed, and his clothes became as bright as a flash of lightning.

Luke 9:28–29

The disciples fail to cast out a demon at the foot of the mountain

"Why couldn't we drive it out?" He replied, "This kind can come out only by prayer."

Mark 9:28–29

Jesus did not pray before exorcising this demon

It takes a life of prayer, a lifestyle of prayer, a lifetime of prayer to confront this kind of evil.

David Garland

VIDEO DISCUSSION #1

1. Looking back at the Bible passages and your video teaching notes, what did you learn that you did not know previously? Consider specifically:

   • Jesus' practice of prayer (Mark 1:32–39)

   • The disciples' failure to understand Jesus' need to pray

   • The disciples' failure to cast out the demon

   • The importance of developing a lifestyle of prayer

   How does this knowledge help you to understand the passages better?

2. Why do you think that Jesus could cast out the demon, but the disciples could not (Mark 9:18, 25, 29)?

3. Do you find prayer an easy or a difficult practice? Why?

GOING DEEPER

Jesus' example in Gethsemane: "Watch and pray"

Video Teaching #2 Notes

Mark 14:32–42: third example of Jesus praying in Mark

> **DID YOU KNOW?**
>
> Gethsemane means "oil press."
>
> Ben Witherington III

> They went to a place called Gethsemane, and Jesus said to his disciples, "Sit here while I pray." He took Peter, James and John along with him.
>
> Mark 14:32–33

Garden of Gethsemane

Peter

James and John

"Watch and pray"

Jesus is distressed in prayer

> He began to be deeply distressed and troubled. "My soul is overwhelmed with sorrow to the point of death." ... Going a little farther, he fell to the ground.
>
> Mark 14:33–35

Those in the will of God may face more formidable forces

My heart is in anguish within me; the terrors of death assail me. Fear and trembling have beset me; horror has overwhelmed me. I said, "Oh, that I had the wings of a dove! I would fly away and be at rest — I would flee far away and stay in the desert; I would hurry to my place of shelter, far from the tempest and storm."

Psalm 55:4–8

Jesus faces the hour, but he faces it in prayer

For Jesus, prayer was not a way to avoid difficulty, but a way to endure it.

Mark Fackler

VIDEO DISCUSSION #2

1. David Garland read a card that said, "Praying really changes things; arranges life anew. It's good for your digestion; gives peaceful sleep at night; and fills the grayest gloomiest day with rays of glowing light." Why do you think that Jesus was not serene and calm in Gethsemane?

2. About to confront his toughest trial, death itself, Jesus faced it with prayer. Do you think that the church today sees prayer as a powerful weapon to face trials and temptations? What evidence have you seen that would support your answer?

3. Because God provides prayer as a weapon to combat sin and also to advance the kingdom, the Devil will fight hard so that we do not pray. Do you think that there is a spiritual battle that takes place whenever we pray? How have you experienced this battle?

CONNECTING THE BIBLE TO LIFE

We can learn from the example of Jesus praying, but we can also learn from the disciples, whose lack of prayer led to failure.

Video Teaching #3 Notes

The disciples' first failure in prayer: inability to drive out a demon (Mark 9)

> The disciples had been tempted to believe that the gift that they had received from Jesus (Mark 6:7) was in their control and could be exercised at their disposal.
>
> William Lane

In prayer we look to God and his power, and not to ourselves

The disciples' second failure in prayer: Gethsemane (Mark 14)

Watch and pray

> "Therefore keep watch because you do not know when the owner of the house will come back.... If he comes suddenly, do not let him find you sleeping. What I say to you, I say to everyone: 'Watch!'"
>
> Mark 13:35–37

When the disciples do not pray ...

A nameless woman anoints Jesus. A bystander carries his cross. A pagan centurion who was there to supervise his execution confesses that he is the son of God. A council member who condemned him to death obtains the body and buries it in his tomb. Women followers watch and go to anoint the body. Male disciples betray, take their rest, flee, and deny — because the flesh is weak, and they do not pray.

David Garland

Our lives are so busy

The danger is ...

> My prayer life became a strategy session during which I informed God about what I intended to accomplish and then asked for blessing with added recommendations about how God could best meet my needs.
>
> Darrell Bock

A lifestyle of prayer

> Epaphras, who is one of you and a servant of Christ Jesus, sends greetings. He is always wrestling in prayer for you, that you may stand firm in all the will of God, mature and fully assured.
>
> Colossians 4:12

> I especially need your prayers because I am (like the pilgrim in Bunyan) traveling across "a plain called Ease." Everything without and many things within are marvelously well.
>
> C. S. Lewis

I am so busy now that if I did not spend two or three hours each day in prayer, I would not get through the day.

Martin Luther

We are going to face those times of testing when we least expect it. The only way for us to be prepared is to be prepared as Jesus was: in a lifetime, lifestyle of prayer with God.

David Garland

VIDEO DISCUSSION #3

1. David Garland said that the lack of prayer in the disciples' lives led to their failures: failure to cast out a demon (Mark 9:18) and failure to be strong when Jesus was arrested (Mark 14:50–52). Why do you think that this is true?

2. Have you ever fallen into the trap of thinking that you need less prayer time than Jesus did? What did you do about it?

3. It is not always possible to get away to a mountain to pray, so we need to learn how to pray in our lives, busy as they are. How can we develop a lifestyle of prayer? What have you personally found that helps you to pray?

MAKING DEEPER CONNECTIONS IN YOUR OWN LIFE

Personal reflection studies to do on your own

Day One *February 3 Thursday*

1. Read Mark 1:32–39.

2. The disciples asked Jesus to "teach [them] to pray" (Luke 11:1) They must have asked him this because they saw Jesus' example of prayer. Would those who know you well know that you are a pray-er? Why or why not?

3. The Jewish Scriptures are filled with prayer. The temple in Jerusalem was known as a house of prayer (Isaiah 56:7). The synagogue was also known as a prayer house. Do you think most people today think of prayer as a characteristic marker of Christians and our churches? Why or why not?

Day Two *Feb. 7 Monday*

1. Read Ephesians 6:10–12, 18–20.

2. Prayer is not just talking—it is also listening. Often it is listening to silence. God never ceases to speak to us, but the voice is frequently drowned out by our busyness and our loud entertainment. Try adding some moments of silence to your life and to your prayer life this week, then journal briefly about the experience.

walking & listening

3. Anyone who tries to pray seriously knows that diabolical interference is inevitable. Why do you think that evil forces would attempt to interrupt or curtail your prayers? Have you found anything that combats that influence in your own life?

Day Three

Feb. 7 Monday

1. Read Mark 9:9–29.

2. While one's posture is not important in prayer, some find that they are better able to express their dependence on God by kneeling when praying, a visible sign of our helplessness apart from divine enablement. Have you tried to pray in different places or at different times of the day or with different body postures? Have you found anything that helps you to pray more attentively?

Bible Reading
Church.

3. Mark 9:9–29 tells us that Jesus was able to cast out the demon without praying. David Garland concludes that Jesus' overall prayer life gave him power when he needed it to do divine work. What about you? Are you investing enough time in prayer so that when difficult times come you are connected to God's strength? What could you do to improve in this area?

Day Four

1. Read Mark 14:32–42.

2. It is interesting that in the final hour, Jesus did not take up arms against the powers of darkness, but instead clasped his hands together in prayer. What is the normal Christian response today to difficulty? Do we begin to pray, or do we begin to try to develop a plan to solve the issue ourselves? How do you think that prayer can really solve difficulties?

    God has a plan if we listen.

3. Once at a home Bible study as the group was sharing their prayer requests, one of the members tapped away at a computer. Asked what he was doing, he replied that he kept a record of the date of the prayer request and when it was answered. The list of prayer requests included a promotion, a mink stole, a vacation cruise, and a date. What are your typical prayer requests? Do they line up with Jesus' model of prayer in the gospel of Mark? Are you praying for kingdom requests?

Day Five

1. Read Mark 1:32–39; 9:9–29; and 14:32–42 one more time.

2. Pray through all three passages, allowing the deeper meaning that you have discovered to lead you as you pray. Ask the Spirit to continue to remind you of what you have learned and to help you apply these truths to your life.

3. Turn back to the discussion questions from the video teaching (Video Discussion #1, #2, #3). If there are questions that your group did not have time to discuss or questions that you might like to think more about, use this time to review and reflect further.

Our God Listens

The Persistent Widow
(Luke 18:1–8)

Dr. Mark Strauss

"Will not God bring about justice for his chosen ones, who cry out to him day and night?"

Luke 18:7

Prayer is to be founded on the goodness of God as a loving parent and lays hold of God's benevolence.

David Garland

INTRODUCTION

Video Opener

Scripture Reading: Luke 18:1–8, followed by a prayer that God will open your heart as you study his Word

Location of Passage: On Jesus' way to Jerusalem, somewhere between the border of Samaria and Galilee (Luke 17:11) and Jericho (Luke 18:35)

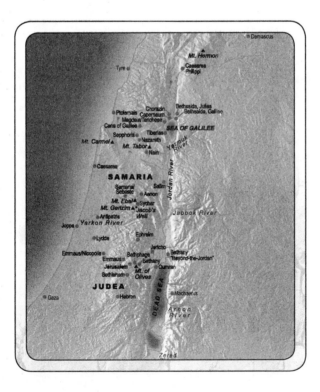

CONNECTING TO THE BIBLE

In contrast to the judge, who is unjust and uncompassionate, God is loving, just, and compassionate.

Video Teaching #1 Notes

Location of Video Teaching: San Diego Superior Courtroom

"The squeaky wheel gets the grease"

> Then Jesus told his disciples a parable to show them that they should always pray and not give up.
>
> Luke 18:1

A widow is under attack

> "Grant me justice against my adversary."
>
> Luke 18:3

The judge

There was a judge who neither feared God nor cared about men.

Luke 18:2

Without money or power, the widow persists

DID YOU KNOW?

The verb is an imperfect tense in Greek, indicating continual action. She did not just go once, the widow *"kept coming again and again"* (Luke 18:3).

The judge grants her justice

"Even though I don't fear God or care about men, yet because this widow keeps bothering me, I will see that she gets justice, so that she won't eventually wear me out with her coming!"

Luke 18:4–5

A teaching about prayer? After all, God is not like this judge.

A Rabbinic argument: "from lesser to greater" (*qal vahomer*).

"And will not God bring about justice for his chosen ones, who cry out to him day and night? Will he keep putting them off? I tell you, he will see that they get justice, and quickly."

Luke 18:7–8

If a wicked man will sometimes do good, even if from bad motives, how much more will God do right!

Leon Morris

A warning for us

The parable teaches two main points

Hulda

VIDEO DISCUSSION #1

1. Looking back at the Bible passage and your video teaching
   notes, what did you learn that you did not know previously?
   Consider specifically:

   page 13 - sumaleon,

   • The judge and the tendency to be corrupt

   • The tenacity of the widow

   God is outside
   time
   God can bend times
   and events in will / however

   • The call for us to pray until the end of time

   How does this knowledge help you to understand the passage
   better?

   If its there for the judge — God even more so.

2. Have you ever been in a situation where the person in power
   would not listen to you? What did you do?

3. Have you ever needed to show tenacity in a situation? Have
   you ever needed to be tenacious in your prayers to God? If so,
   explain one such situation to the other group members.

   working 11 years to settle with Lepawsky.

GOING DEEPER

In order to fully understand the parable of the persistent widow, we must understand its two key characters — the widow and the judge — in their first-century context.

no father
no sons.

Video Teaching #2 Notes

persistent
winning
Is 1: 17

The widow

destitute
powerless
not protected
vulnerable
helpless

no one
is pleading
her case.
persistence
wins out.

Widows in our culture

Widows in the first-century context: powerless

Learn to do right! Seek justice, encourage the oppressed. Defend the cause of the fatherless, plead the case of the widow.

Isaiah 1:17

— ☯ —

Religion that God our Father accepts as pure and faultless is this: to look after orphans and widows in their distress.

James 1:27

She goes to the judge alone

She has two strikes against her, yet ...

> The language Luke uses is startling, perhaps even humorous, for it
> invokes images of the almighty, fearless, macho judge cornered and
> slugged by the least powerful in society.
>
> Joel Green

The judge

Judges in our culture

Judges in the first century

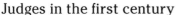

honour & shame good.

> [Jehoshaphat] appointed judges in the land ... of Judah. He told them, "... Now let the fear of the LORD be upon you. Judge carefully, for with the LORD our God there is no injustice or partiality or bribery."
>
> 2 Chronicles 19:5–7

DID YOU KNOW?

Judges in Jerusalem were called Dayyaney Gezeroth ("judges of prohibitions or punishment"). Later rabbis made a play on these words; they called them Dayyaney Gezeloth ("judges of thievery") because they perverted justice through bribery.

Judges were to fear God and therefore defend the oppressed. Many ancient societies had severe legal penalties for unjust judges.

Craig Keener

Judges often abused the system in the first century

The Talmud speaks of village judges who were so easily bribed that they were willing to pervert justice for a dish of meat.

B. T. Baba Kamma 114a

An honor-shame culture

God is *not* like the judge

> What Jesus has highlighted in his example and emphasized in his
> teaching about prayer is the goodness of the Father.
>
> I. H. Marshall

VIDEO DISCUSSION #2

1. Why do you think that the widow did not just give up when she saw that the judge "neither feared God nor cared about men" (Luke 18:2–3)?

2. Why do you think that the judge finally gave in and granted the widow's request (vv. 4–5)?

3. What do you think this parable teaches us about God (vv. 6–8)?

CONNECTING THE BIBLE TO LIFE

Does God want us to wear him down, to give him a black eye? Is this what the parable teaches us about prayer?

Video Teaching #3 Notes

Getting in line with God's purposes, through prayer

> Pray continually.
>
> 1 Thessalonians 5:17
>
> Pray in the Spirit on all occasions.
>
> Ephesians 6:18

Getting to know God through prayer

It's not about our needs; it's about his will

Delight yourself in the LORD and he will give you the desires of your heart.

Psalm 37:4

In prayer we should draw ourselves to God and not try to pull God down to us.

David Garland

Jesus learned God's will through prayer

The Lord's Prayer: it's about his will

Our faith grows through adversity

"When the Son of Man comes, will he find faith on the earth?"

Luke 18:8

This parable is not about us; it's about God

> Since ancient times no one has heard, no ear has perceived, no eye has seen any God besides you, who acts on behalf of those who wait for him. You come to the help of those who gladly do right, who remember your ways.
>
> Isaiah 64:4–5

VIDEO DISCUSSION #3

1. How do you think Luke 18:8 relates to the rest of Jesus' parable (vv. 1–7)?

   faith on the earth.
   what is God's
   purpose?

2. Mark Strauss closed by saying that the parable is not about us, but about God. What did you learn in this parable about the importance of finding God's will? How can we be sure that this knowledge doesn't just stay in our heads but changes our lives?

MAKING DEEPER CONNECTIONS IN YOUR OWN LIFE

Personal reflection studies to do on your own

Day One

1. Read Acts 4:23–31.

2. Two students on a college campus were recently discussing why they do not pray more often. Their response: "I don't think that we really believe that prayer works, otherwise we would pray much more." This parable assures us that prayer is indeed effective, and that we are to continue to pray in faith for God to act. Reflect on your own prayer life. What keeps you from praying?

3. Think about prayer times that you have had recently, or those in your church. Do they attempt to "wear God down" with requests for vindication and justice? Or have they fallen into the trap of asking for the same old things? This parable teaches us that we are to persist in faithful prayer that God would act according to his character (consider also the prayer recorded in today's reading). Take some time praying to God that he would show himself through you today. Record your prayer or highlights of it here.

Day Two

1. Read Matthew 7:7–11.

2. The Luke 18 parable assures us that God truly cares for us. If human fathers know how to give good gifts to their children, how much more so our loving, heavenly Father (Matthew 7:11). Journal briefly about the nature of God and his love and concern for you. Ask him to comfort your heart with the truth that he cares more for your life than you do.

3. What "good gifts" would you like to receive from God through prayer (Matthew 7:11)? Read Luke 11:13 and compare it to Matthew 7:11. Why do you think Luke uses the "Holy Spirit" whereas Matthew uses "good gifts"?

   People can give good gifts but Jesus gave Holy Spirit

Day Three

1. Read Isaiah 64:1–12.

2. Most people want justice right away. This parable reminds us that we may not get full vindication until the Son of Man comes again (see Luke 18:8). Do you ever struggle persisting in obedience and prayer despite the present circumstances? Read through Revelation 19 to remind yourself of God's ultimate victory in the world.

3. Because of the recent increase in terrorism, there is more discussion about when and how the end times will come. The Luke text encourages us to remember that our duty as disciples of Christ is to live faithfully in patient expectation of Jesus' return. Spend some time in prayer, asking God to show you how you can remain faithful today. Journal your thoughts.

Day Four

1. Read Isaiah 47:8–11.

2. The fact that the Luke 18 parable tells about a judge who did not give justice to a widow should not be overlooked. As Christians we are called to care for social outcasts, even if they have nothing to offer us in return. Pray today specifically for those who are the neediest in the world, asking God to show you what role you might play in bringing justice to these people.

3. Craig Blomberg (*Preaching the Parables*, 175–76) asks why we don't hear more talk in our American evangelical churches about persecuted churches and people in the world, instead of the typical set of social issues such as abortion, homosexuality, prayer in the schools, and creation versus evolution. He asks, "Why don't we hear an appeal for Christians to eat out less, to waste less food and less gasoline, to stop going into such enormous debt with money that could be better spent?" Why do you think the American church does not talk about or pray more about these social issues of injustice?

Day Five

1. Read Luke 18:1–8 one more time.

2. Pray through the entire passage verse by verse, allowing the deeper meaning that you have discovered to lead you as you pray. Ask the Spirit to continue to remind you of what you have learned and to help you apply these truths to your life.

3. Turn back to the discussion questions from the video teaching (Video Discussion #1, #2, #3). If there are questions that your group did not have time to discuss or questions that you might like to think more about, use this time to review and reflect further.

SESSION 3

Joining in Jesus' Prayer

The Lord's Prayer
(Matthew 6:9–13)

Dr. Michael Wilkins

"This, then, is how you should pray: 'Our Father in heaven ...' "

🙠 *Matthew 6:9*

Jesus invites us to share in the prayer-life of Jesus himself.

🙠 *N. T. Wright*

47

INTRODUCTION

Video Opener

Scripture Reading: Matthew 6:5 – 13 (vv. 5 – 8 provide the context for the Lord's Prayer), followed by a prayer that God will open your heart as you study his Word

Location of Prayer: The traditional site of the Lord's Prayer is west of Capernaum, at present-day Tabgha.

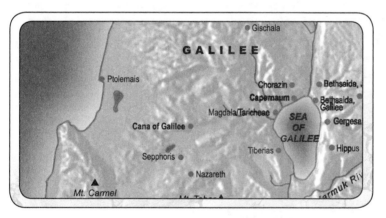

Tabgha, the Sea of Galilee

CONNECTING TO THE BIBLE

Jesus teaches his disciples how to pray in a way that gives glory to God and gives profound meaning to their requests. This really is the "disciples' prayer" since Jesus invites the disciples to join with him in his own prayer life.

Video Teaching #1 Notes

Location of Video Teaching: San Onofre State Park, San Clemente, California

The geographical setting of the Lord's Prayer (Sermon on Mount)

> Now when he saw the crowds, he went up on a mountainside and sat down. His disciples came to him, and he began to teach them.
>
> Matthew 5:1–2

The social setting of the Lord's Prayer

> "And when you pray, do not be like the hypocrites, for they love to pray standing in the synagogues and on the street corners to be seen by men.... And when you pray, do not keep on babbling like pagans, for they think they will be heard because of their many words."
>
> Matthew 6:5, 7

The structure of the prayer

The invocation: "Our Father in heaven" (Matthew 6:9)

Abba - our heavenly Father;
Jesus invites people
into an intimate
relationship with God.

> "Our Father, merciful Father"; "Graciously favor us, our Father, with understanding from you"; "Forgive us, our Father, for we have sinned against you."
>
> Sample Jewish prayers

First petition: "Hallowed be your name" (v. 9)

Let your name
be Holy

> Exalted and hallowed be his great name in the world which he created according to his will.
>
> Jewish *Káddish*

> It is when God's people live holy lives that the world will see God as holy. (See Ezekiel 36:20–23.)

Second petition: "Your kingdom come" (v. 10)

[handwritten notes]

> When Christians pray "Your kingdom come" they are praying for the completion of a kingdom which has already come with Jesus.
>
> Oscar Cullmann

Third petition: "Your will be done on earth as it is in heaven" (v. 10)

[handwritten notes]

The shift from focusing on God to focusing on our needs

[handwritten notes]

Fourth petition: "Give us today our daily bread" (v. 11)

[handwritten notes]

DID YOU KNOW?

The term "bread" has multiple meanings. In antiquity "bread" was never taken as something merely material.

Robert Karris

Fifth petition: "Forgive us our debts" (v. 12)

Forgive us our *debts*, as we also have forgiven our debtors.

Matthew 6:12

Forgive us our *sins*.

Luke 11:4

Forgive your neighbor the wrong he has done, and then your sins will be pardoned when you pray.

Sirach 28:2

"Drink from it, all of you. This is my blood of the covenant, which is poured out for many for the forgiveness of sins."

Matthew 26:27–28

Sixth petition: "And lead us not into temptation, but deliver us from the evil one" (v. 13)

Remove tests and we are caught between Jesus & the evil one.

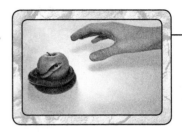

When tempted, no one should say, "God is tempting me." For God cannot be tempted by evil, nor does he tempt anyone.

James 1:13

Liturgical ending: "For thine is the kingdom, and the power, and the glory forever, Amen"

VIDEO DISCUSSION #1

1. Looking back at the Bible passage and your video teaching notes, what did you learn that you did not know previously? Consider specifically:

   • The setting of the Lord's Prayer

   • The structure of the Lord's Prayer

   • The meaning of each one of the six petitions

   • The liturgical ending

   How does this knowledge help you to understand the prayer better?

2. Do you think that we should recite the Lord's Prayer word for word, or is it simply a model prayer that gives structure to our prayer lives?

3. What is the significance of the order of the Lord's Prayer, beginning with three petitions that address God (Matthew 6:9–10) and then ending with three petitions that address our own needs (vv. 11–13)?

GOING DEEPER

The Jews were a praying people. The Lord's Prayer has roots in the Old Testament and in other Jewish prayers of Jesus' day. The temple and synagogue were known as places of prayer and not just places of sacrifice or fellowship.

Video Teaching #2 Notes

God's name (Matthew 6:9)

> **DID YOU KNOW?**
>
> The term "Father" is used with reference to God in the Old Testament 40 times; but in the New Testament 260 times. Jesus has radically changed the believer's view of God as "Father."
>
> I. H. Marshall

Exalted and hallowed be his great name in the world which he created according to his will.

Jewish *Káddish*

God's kingdom (v. 10)

> May he rule his kingdom in your lifetime and in your days and in the lifetime of the whole house of Israel, speedily and soon.
>
> Jewish *Káddish*

God's will (v. 10)

> "I desire to do your will, O my God; your law is within my heart."
>
> Psalm 40:8

———— ◉ ————

> "My food ... is to do the will of him who sent me and to finish his work."
>
> John 4:34

———— ◉ ————

> "My Father, if it is possible, may this cup be taken from me. Yet not as I will, but as you will."
>
> Matthew 26:39 (see also v. 42)

Disciples carried out God's will

The complete experience of God's will on earth occurs only when his kingdom comes to earth in its final form, causing an overthrow of all evil rule. (See Revelation 20:1 – 10.)

Our nourishment (v. 11)

"I will rain down bread from heaven for you. The people are to go out each day and gather enough for that day." ... However, some of them paid no attention to Moses; they kept part of it until morning, but it was full of maggots and began to smell.

Exodus 16:4, 20

The prayer is for our needs, not our greeds.

D. A. Carson

He only denounces his disciples' *anxiety* about the future, not responsible care for the future.

Michael Wilkins

Forgiveness of our debts or sins (v. 12)

DID YOU KNOW?

The same Aramaic word could be used for both the Greek words "sins" and "debts."

Craig Keener

Our spiritual battle (v. 13)

Rely on God to do the battle.

"Watch and pray so that you will not fall into temptation."

Matthew 26:41

Bring me not into the power of sin,
And not into the power of guilt,
And not into the power of temptation,
And not into the power of anything shameful.

b. Berakoth 60b

VIDEO DISCUSSION #2

1. The Lord's Prayer teaches us to call God Abba, "Father," which expresses intimacy with him — he is our friend. However, Abba also has another connotation: the "Father" was the authority. When we call God "Father," we need to remember both intimacy and authority. Which of these two aspects do you think the church emphasizes today? What happens when we emphasize just one aspect of the nature of the "Father"?

2. The Lord's Prayer teaches us to trust God on a daily basis as we ask for our "daily" bread (Matthew 6:11). We are not taught to pray for our needs for the next ten years, but for "today." What might this principle of trust and faith teach us in a society that has so many financial problems, where even Christians are going deep into debt and having problems with being content (Philippians 4:11)?

CONNECTING THE BIBLE TO LIFE

The Lord's Prayer is far more than just a liturgical practice to be repeated in church. It leads us into the very heart of God and provides a paradigm for developing discipleship to Jesus in every area of life.

Video Teaching #3 Notes

An invitation to pray

greater intimacy
with Him &
other believers
should feel way to
help on each
other.
This prayer is
a model.

A model prayer

Setting right priorities

[handwritten notes]
First 3 on God
value on His name
Kingdom.

> "Seek first his kingdom and his righteousness, and all these things will be given to you as well."
>
> Matthew 6:33

We are taught to pray in the first person plural: "us," "we," and "our." The Lord's Prayer never leads to individualistic praying.

Michael Wilkins

A relationship with our Father in heaven

[handwritten notes]
friend
comforter
authority
He impacts on all
fronts.
He cares about His.
will for our lives.

He wishes to be called Father rather than Lord, so that he may give us great confidence in seeking him and great help in beseeching him.

Anonymous

All the prayer's petitions are based in this relationship (in wanting God's will)

> When we know God as our Father, we understand that he cares about his will for our lives even more than we do. To place our lives in his hands means that he will always bring about what is best for us, even when it may mean sacrifice, or hardship, or difficult times.
>
> Michael Wilkins

Hope for those without an earthly father

He provides guidance where there is an emptiness.

The Lord's Prayer is a paradigm for discipleship

Find real life in the Father's name

> People who pray for the coming of the kingdom of God rightly pray that the kingdom of God might be established in them.
>
> Origen, an early church father

VIDEO DISCUSSION #3

1. Many people shrink back because of the high cost of following God's will. Wherever God leads, however, is where we will find ultimate peace and joy, even if that means that suffering will be involved. Can you remember a time when you followed God's will when it was difficult and then discovered that it led to joy? How about remembering a time when you thought that it was too hard to follow God's will, so you decided not to do it?

2. The Lord's Prayer reminds us that we must first seek his kingdom and then seek our needs. What do you think would happen in your life or in the life of the church if we followed these priorities? Do we place God first in our prayers, or do we jump right to our own personal list of wants from God?

MAKING DEEPER CONNECTIONS IN YOUR OWN LIFE

Personal reflection studies to do on your own

Day One

[handwritten: Be holy because I am holy.]

1. Read Leviticus 20:7–8; Deuteronomy 14:1–2; 1 Peter 1:15–16.

2. "Hallowed be your name," literally "may your name be seen as holy" (Matthew 6:9), reminds us that God is inflexibly holy. He is not just our friend or "buddy." Reflect on the holiness of God and his grace in accepting us as unholy creations. Write out your own prayer of worship and thanksgiving.

[handwritten: Thank you God for the sacrifice of Christ. Thank you that you are our High Priest, have given us the Holy Ghost. You alone are worthy. You promise us eternal life.]

3. It is when God's people live holy lives that the world sees God as holy. The Old Testament looked forward to the day when God would show himself holy *through* his people. Read Ezekiel 36:23–27. The Spirit has now come, and we are "the light of the world" (Matthew 5:14). Is the Spirit's power (Ephesians 3:16–20) helping you to become more holy? Is your holy "light" shining to the world so that they "see your good deeds and praise your Father in heaven" (Matthew 5:16)?

[handwritten: We are justified by faith not the Law.]

[handwritten: 1 adoration, 2 supplication, 3 confession, Our Father, Lord's prayer, temptation, protection]

Day Two

1. Read Luke 11:1–4, and compare and contrast this passage with Matthew 6:9–13.

[handwritten: Our father, Our father which be on earth your will be done, forgive our sins our debts, deliver us from the evil one]

2. While some try to have a set prayer time each day, others have a more varied prayer life. While some pray while sitting, others find that kneeling or standing helps them to concentrate better. What are you doing that is helping your prayer life? What are you not doing that you might like to try?

> setting a daily time
> doing going to a Bible study.

3. Jesus has given us a model prayer. This does not mean that we should simply repeat this prayer over and over again. Rather, it teaches us basic principles of how a Christian should pray (such as the priority of putting God before our own needs). What do you think Matthew 6:9–13 is teaching you about your own prayer life?

Day Three

1. Read Romans 8:1–5.   minds set on what the Spirit desires

2. Jesus taught that we should pray for the Father's help to avoid temptations by the Evil One (Matthew 6:13). Spend some time reflecting on your areas of weakness and praying that the Father would help you overcome these areas so that you can better reflect his holiness. Record your thoughts.

> Poor me syndrome – weak tired fed up

3. Implicit in the prayer that God's "will be done" (Matthew 6:10) is the admission that it is not always being done. Would you say that the Christians you know totally follow God's will, or do they struggle? What difference does knowing Jesus make in your life in terms of obedience?

Knowing what Christ would do WWCD perfect leader to follow.

4. While the Lord's Prayer does not teach us that our forgiveness from God is dependent on our forgiveness of others, it does remind us that those who have been forgiven forgive others (Matthew 6:12). Reflect on your relationships in your church, your neighborhood, your workplace, your school. Are there people who you need to forgive? Are there people who need to forgive you? *Yes.*

Day Four

1. Read Romans 8:26–27 and Ephesians 6:18–20.

2. The Lord's Prayer teaches us to pray in the first person plural: "us," "we," and "our." Do you remember the needs of others in your prayers, or just your own needs? Spend some time praying for others.

Barbara's friend Laura Mallory Smith, Tamara.

3. The context of the Lord's Prayer includes a rebuke of hypocritical Jewish pray-ers who pray to be seen by others (Matthew 6:5). Our prayers, Jesus says, should be done in secret (v. 6). While this does not mean that we should never pray in public, it does teach us two things. First, when we pray in public, we should be sure that we are praying to God and not to those who are listening to us. Second, we should have a secret prayer life. How are you doing in these two areas?

Day Five

1. Read Matthew 6:9–13 one more time.

2. Pray through the entire passage verse by verse, allowing the deeper meaning that you have discovered to lead you as you pray. Ask the Spirit to continue to remind you of what you have learned and to help you apply these truths to your life.

3. Turn back to the discussion questions from the video teaching (Video Discussion #1, #2, #3). If there are questions that your group did not have time to discuss or questions that you might like to think more about, use this time to review and reflect further.

Praying to a Good God

The Friend at Midnight
(Luke 11:5–13)

Dr. Ben Witherington III

"If you then, though you are evil, know how to give good gifts to your children, how much more will your Father in heaven give the Holy Spirit to those who ask him!"

@ Luke 11:13

What Jesus has emphasized in his teaching about prayer is the goodness of the Father.

@ I. H. Marshall

INTRODUCTION

Video Opener

Scripture Reading: Luke 11:5–13, followed by a prayer that God will open your heart as you study his Word

Location of Teaching: Exact location unknown (Luke 11:1); probably in Galilee, on Jesus' way to Jerusalem (9:51), preaching in small towns and villages (13:22); near the home of Mary and Martha in Bethany (10:38)

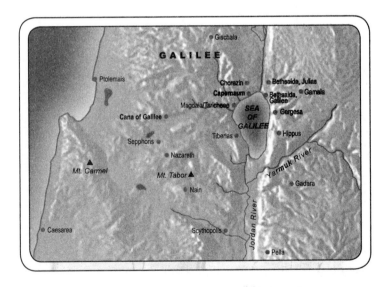

CONNECTING TO THE BIBLE

This parable teaches us to persist and even to be bold in asking God for anything.

Video Teaching #1 Notes

Location of Video Teaching: Heartbreak Hill, on the Boston Marathon course

Reading the parable of the friend at midnight

What is this parable telling us about God?

A relationship

Hospitality in that culture

Shame

Shame would come upon the whole village — not just on the friend — if he offered mere subsistence.

M. M. B. Turner

God is ready to give

Friends come through for us despite inconvenience to themselves, and sometimes despite mixed motives for their goodness. How much more can we be confident that God will come through for us.

John Nolland

"If you then, though you are evil, know how to give ... how much more will your Father in heaven give ..."

Luke 11:13

VIDEO DISCUSSION #1

1. Looking back at the Bible passage and your video teaching notes, what did you learn that you did not know previously? Consider specifically:

   • God's readiness to give

   • The importance of relationship in prayer

   • Shame

   • Hospitality

   How does this knowledge help you to understand the prayer better?

2. If there are any parents in your group, have them discuss their own attitude toward their children when they are asked for something. Do they want to give good gifts to their children or do they want to withhold from them? What could this tell us about God?

3. When you pray, do you envision God as one who is ready to give or reluctant to give? Explain.

VIBRANT
VIGOROUS
PRAYER

GOING DEEPER

We will understand more deeply what Jesus is telling us about asking, seeking, and knocking on heaven's door when we understand shame and prayer in the Near Eastern culture.

Video Teaching #2 Notes

Houses in ancient Near Eastern culture

Honor and shame in ancient Near Eastern culture

> The parable tells of a sleeping neighbor who will indeed preserve his honor and grant the friend's request and more.
>
> Kenneth Bailey

Prayer in ancient Near Eastern culture

> One day Jesus was praying in a certain place. When he finished, one of his disciples said to him, "Lord, teach us to pray."
>
> Luke 11:1

The type of prayer Jesus is calling us to

> If we do not want what we are asking for enough to be persistent, we do not want it very much.
>
> Leon Morris

Boldness in prayer

"Good things" (Matthew) or "the Holy Spirit" (Luke)

> God gives us every "good gift" (Matthew 7:11), but the greatest gift that God can give us is the Spirit (Luke 11:13).

"Ask ... seek ... knock" (Luke 11:9)

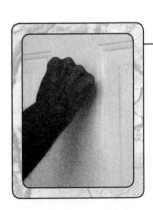

VIDEO DISCUSSION #2

1. Can God be "shamed" into answering our prayers? What is this parable trying to teach us about the nature of God?

2. Why do you think that Matthew says that God will give us "good gifts," but Luke says he will give us the "Holy Spirit?"

CONNECTING THE BIBLE TO LIFE

Prayer is not just about petition, it's about communion with God in an ongoing personal relationship.

Video Teaching #3 Notes

John Kelley and the Boston Marathon

The marathon: a spiritual experience

provisions along the way.

{ extra strength
{ extra resources

Praying for big things, the Holy Spirit

God is a better friend

> People ought not to think of God as unwilling to give: he is always ready to give good gifts to his people. But it is important that they do their part by asking.
>
> Leon Morris

We can pray whenever we want

We should expect results

VIDEO DISCUSSION #3

1. Based on our experiences in life, we might have thoughts and feelings about God that are different than the biblical picture. Do you envision God as one who wants to give you "good gifts" (Luke 11:13)? Do you envision him as more willing to give you good gifts than your very best friend? Why or why not?

2. The fact that the man goes to his friend at midnight helps us to understand that we can go to God in prayer at any time of the day or night. Do you pray throughout the day, or just during a set devotional time? What benefits could there be to praying throughout the day?

MAKING DEEPER CONNECTIONS IN YOUR OWN LIFE

Personal reflection studies to do on your own

Day One

1. Read Romans 8:30–39.

2. God is sometimes seen as a mean father, but the Scriptures teach a different view. It is important to understand the truth about the goodness of God if we are going to be motivated to pray to him as a good Father. Reflect on the goodness of God as found in such texts as Romans 8:30–39 and Luke 11:5–13. If you have time, skim through other passages of Scripture and use a journal to keep a list of the qualities of God.

    Rom. 8:34
    Who shall separate us from God?
    Shall trouble or hardship or persecution or famine or nakedness or danger or sword
    No.

3. In addition to knowing about the good qualities of God the Father, it is also important to spend time with him. Pray through the qualities of God and spend time with him as you seek to build a deeper relationship.

Day Two

The prayer of a righteous man is powerful + effective

1. Read James 5:16 and 1 Peter 3:12.

    The eyes of the Lord are on the righteous.

2. James seems to connect forgiveness of sins and answered prayer. Peter seems to connect righteousness with answered prayer. Do you think that there is a relationship between your own righteousness and God's willingness to answer your prayers? Why or why not?

    no, God decides not me

3. Darrell Bock writes: "Not praying is like walking up to the marriage altar, saying one's vows, and then going mute as the relationship moves forward from day to day" (*Luke,* NIVAC, 312). In others words, prayer should be a normal part of a relationship with God. Do you find this to be true in your relationship with God?

Day Three

Peter . when you have turned back strengthen your brother.

1. Read Luke 22:32.

2. God expects us to be bold in our requests to him, understanding that our boldness does not guarantee that we always get what *we* want. What do you think is the relationship between God's will and our boldness and persistence in prayer? Do you think that your prayers make a difference in the world? Why or why not?

3. While Luke 11 teaches us to be bold in our prayers to God, Luke 22:32 reminds us that Jesus is also praying for us (read Hebrews 7:25). What difference does it make in your own prayer life to be assured that Jesus the High Priest is praying that you do not fall?

Christ lives to intercede for us.

Day Four

1. Read Psalm 55.

But as for me, I trust in you.

2. Psalm 55 reminds us that in prayer we can be honest to God about our need for help and deliverance. Consider any difficult areas in your life, and then pray about them as you remember the lesson of boldness that the friend at midnight had as he went to his friend for three loaves of bread. Journal your thoughts.

3. If your experience with your earthly father was not good, it might be more difficult for you to accept that God your heavenly Father is good and wants to give you good gifts. If this is your situation, ask God to help you understand his true, divine nature. If your earthly father was good to you, thank God for that and ask him to show you how he is even better than your earthly father.

Day Five

1. Read Luke 11:5–13 one more time.

2. Pray through the entire passage verse by verse, allowing the deeper meaning that you have discovered to lead you as you pray. Ask the Spirit to continue to remind you of what you have learned and to help you apply these truths to your life.

3. Turn back to the discussion questions from the video teaching (Video Discussion #1, #2, #3). If there are questions that your group did not have time to discuss or questions that you might like to think more about, use this time to review and reflect further.

SESSION 5

Praying with Purpose

Jesus' Final Prayer
(John 17)

Dr. Gary Burge

"I pray also for those who will believe in me through their message, that all of them may be one, Father, just as you are in me and I am in you."

John 17:20 – 21

If you really want to know someone's heart, listen to them pray.

Michael Card

INTRODUCTION

Video Opener

Scripture Reading: John 17, followed by a prayer that God will open your heart as you study his Word

Location of Prayer: Jerusalem, either in the Upper Room, or on Jesus' way to the Garden of Gethsemane (John 14:31), perhaps in the Temple courts

Twelfth-century Gothic room built upon the traditional location of the Upper Room

CONNECTING TO THE BIBLE

Through his prayer in John 17, Jesus teaches how the church can succeed in the world. In this prayer we have a glimpse into the very heart of Jesus.

Video Teaching #1 Notes

Location of Video Teaching: Abandoned church, Chicago suburbs

John 17: Jesus' farewell prayer

Jesus prays for the survival of the church

Model of Jerusalem temple

Part 1: Jesus prays for his glorification (John 17:1–8)

"And now, Father, glorify me in your presence with the glory I had with you before the world began."

John 17:5

The Old Testament says that God will not give his glory to another. Jesus' sharing his Father's glory thus implies that he is God.

Andreas Köstenberger

"For I gave them the words you gave me and they accepted them."

John 17:8

In his death, he can glorify God

VIDEO DISCUSSION #1

1. Looking back at the Bible passage and your video teaching notes, what did you learn that you did not know previously? Consider specifically:

   • The location of the prayer

   • The importance of Jesus bringing glory to God

   • Audible prayers in Judaism

   How does this knowledge help you to understand the prayer better?

2. Gary Burge said, "Throughout his life Jesus demonstrated the glory of God by letting people see the reality of God in his own heart (John 1:14; 2:11; 11:4, 40). When people saw this, they could gain eternal life." What does this look like for us? How can we show others the reality of God in our lives so that God is glorified as they find eternal life through Jesus?

3. Even though Jesus prayed that he would glorify God in his death, Gethsemane shows us that the road of suffering was not easy for him. What role do you think prayer has in the life of one who is suffering?

GOING DEEPER

While Jesus was in the world, he could protect his followers from the hostilities of the world's darkness (John 17:12). But now they will be on their own. This is the hidden anxiety in the prayer.

Video Teaching #2 Notes

Part 2: Jesus prays for his disciples (John 17:9–19)

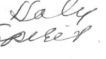

"I pray for them. I am not praying for the world, but for those you have given me."

John 17:9

First, Jesus prays that his followers will obey God's word

 "I have given them your word."

John 17:14

Second, Jesus prays that his followers will be protected from Satan

"My prayer is not that you take them out of the world but that you protect them from the evil one."

John 17:15

The extent of God's protection over us every single day is beyond our comprehension.

Bruce Barton

"Holy Father, protect them by the power of your *name*."

John 17:11

The *name* of the LORD is a strong tower; the righteous run to it and are safe.

Proverbs 18:10

DID YOU KNOW?

In the ancient world, a person's name stood for who the person was and what the person represented.

Richard Longenecker

Third, Jesus prays that his followers will be holy

"Sanctify them by the truth; your word is truth."

John 17:17

"For them I sanctify myself, that they too may be truly sanctified."

John 17:19

The address "Holy Father" in 17:11 would suggest to the Jewish mind that holiness was also expected of Jesus' followers.

Andreas Köstenberger

Part 3: Jesus prays for the church (John 17:20–26)

First, Jesus prays for unity

Unity is beyond human ability

"May they be brought to complete unity to let the world know that you sent me and have loved them even as you have loved me."

John 17:23

Second, Jesus prays that we will see his full glory

"Father, I want those you have given me to be with me where I am, and to see my glory, the glory you have given me because you loved me before the creation of the world."

John 17:24

One assignment: love

> The basis of the unity of the Church is the nature of God and the reality of his redemptive activity. More specifically, it is an outflow of the relations within the Triune God.
>
> George Beasley-Murray

God desires relationship

VIDEO DISCUSSION #2

1. Gary Burge said that our holiness comes about through Jesus' death. This is true on two different levels. First, Jesus' death provides us with holy standing before the Father (justification). Second, in his death, Jesus also gives the Holy Spirit, who empowers us to live holy lives (sanctification). How do justification and sanctification relate to one another? Which of the two do you think is emphasized more in your church?

2. Gary Burge said that God desires a relationship with us. He said that "when we have intimacy and conversation with the Father, it will give new birth to our walk with God." What do you think Gary Burge means by this? Have you experienced this in your life?

CONNECTING THE BIBLE TO LIFE

We are the subjects of Jesus' prayer in John 17. Jesus is our Lord and Shepherd just as he was the Lord and Shepherd of the small circle of men in the Upper Room.

Video Teaching #3 Notes

Jesus' outlook—our outlook

> "Father, I want those you have given me to be with me where I am, and to see my glory."
>
> John 17:24

The cross was to be not a defeat but a victory.

Leon Morris

Jesus' hopes for the church

God's reality

Truth

> "Sanctify them by the truth; your word is truth."
>
> John 17:17

Community

John 17 : 20 − 23.

> "That all of them may be one, Father, just as you are in me and I am in you."
>
> John 17:21

Unity among believers is grounded in the love and unity that exists among the Godhead: God the Father, Jesus the Son, and the Holy Spirit

The church's agenda/mission

VIDEO DISCUSSION #3

1. Jesus not only is preparing a place for us (John 14:3) but he is eager for us to join him there, to see his glory, and to witness the tremendous love the Father has for him (and us). How would our living and our praying change if our minds were filled with such a vision?

2. What do you think Gary Burge meant when he said that people are looking for religious experiences, but that these experiences must be anchored in the truth of God's Word? Do you think that the church today looks more to "experiences" or to "truth"? What are the problems with overemphasizing one at the expense of the other?

3. Jesus teaches in this prayer that Christian holiness, love, and unity are not an end in themselves but the means by which we may reach the lost world for him (John 17:21, 23). This means that those who are living out the love and unity of Christ should be attracting new members to their community. Have you seen this type of growth in your church community? Why or why not?

MAKING DEEPER CONNECTIONS IN YOUR OWN LIFE

Personal reflection studies to do on your own

Day One

1. Read John 17:11, 20–23.

2. If unity attracts people to God and Christianity (John 17:21, 23), a lack of unity has the opposite effect. How could you build unity in your church community?

   How would the church be if everyone was like me?

3. Now, on a broader scale: how can your church build unity among the Christians in your town/city so that the Christian witness in your area is improved? Think about such things as a citywide pastors' group; sporting events; corporate worship gatherings; shared ministries, and so on.

   yes.

Day Two

1. Read John 17:1–5.

2. Reflect on the overall purpose of Jesus' prayer in John 17. Above all, he was interested in God's glory, which would be magnified through Christians who live in unity, love, and obedience. How could you make these same characteristics higher priorities in your life?

3. Reflect on the pattern of Jesus' prayer in John 17. He prayed first for God's glory and his own glory (17:1–8), then for those closest to him (17:9–19), and then for those he did not know (17:20–26). How could this pattern provide help for your own prayer life?

Day Three

1. Read John 17:13–19, 24.

2. John 17:3 says, "Now this is eternal life: that they may know you, the only true God, and Jesus Christ, whom you have sent." The verb "to know" in Greek means not just head knowledge, but a relationship. Are you more interested in trying to accumulate mere information about God or in having a relationship with him? Why?

3. We see throughout this prayer that Jesus looks beyond his imminent suffering to the glory awaiting him in heaven. If you were able to have a heavenly focus, as Jesus taught in this prayer (John 17:5, 13), how would it change your attitude toward things here on earth? How would it transform your own difficulties and suffering?

4. Imagine that doctors had just told you that you have an illness which would lead to your certain death in seven days. You are surrounded by your family and closest friends. What would you tell them? How would you make your final farewell?

How much I love them

Day Four

1. Read John 17:9, 15, 20 and Hebrews 7:24–27.

2. Jesus' sanctification "for" others involved self-sacrifice (John 17:19; Hebrews 7:27). Does the process of sanctification that is taking place in your own life involve self-sacrifice or was that unique to Jesus' experience? Explain.

3. Reflect on the comfort that can be yours knowing that Jesus prayed (John 17:20) and is presently praying for you (Hebrews 7:25). *Jesus always lives to intercedes for us*

Day Five

1. Read John 17 one more time.

2. Pray through the entire passage verse by verse, allowing the deeper meaning that you have discovered to lead you as you pray. Ask the Spirit to continue to remind you of what you have learned and to help you apply these truths to your life.

3. Turn back to the discussion questions from the video teaching (Video Discussion #1, #2, #3). If there are questions that your group did not have time to discuss or questions that you might like to think more about, use this time to review and reflect further.

A Friend in High Places

Faith, Prayer, and Answers
(John 14:13–14)

Dr. Matt Williams

"I will do whatever you ask in my name."

John 14:13

Prayer is not conquering God's reluctance but laying hold of God's willingness.

Neil Anderson

INTRODUCTION

Video Opener

Scripture Reading: John 14:13–14, followed by a prayer that God will open your heart as you study his Word

Location of Passage: Jerusalem, in the Upper Room

Twelfth-century Gothic room built upon the traditional location of the Upper Room

CONNECTING TO THE BIBLE

We often pray for family, for neighbors, for cancer to be healed, for finances ... the list is endless. But God is silent. How do we reconcile that with this great promise of Jesus in John 14, "I will do whatever you ask in my name"?

Video Teaching #1 Notes

Location of Video Teaching: Mission of San Diego de Alcalá

The "problem" of God's silence

Jesus' great promise of answered prayer

DID YOU KNOW?

There are 59,711 books listed on Amazon.com under the subject of prayer, 7,069 of which are about "how to pray."

"I will do whatever you *ask* in my name."	John 14:13
"You may *ask* me for anything in my name, and I will do it."	John 14:14
"*Ask* whatever you wish, and it will be given you."	John 15:7
"The Father will give you whatever you *ask* in my name."	John 15:16
"My Father will give you whatever you *ask* in my name."	John 16:23
"*Ask* and you will receive."	John 16:24

Theme 1: prayer for help to continue Jesus' work

God sends Jesus to do his work

actions &
teaching
to complete God's work
on earth.

> "I have brought you glory on earth by completing the work you gave me to do."
>
> John 17:4
>
>
>
> These [signs] are written that you may believe that Jesus is the Christ, the Son of God, and that by believing you may have life in his name.
>
> John 20:31

Jesus sends us to continue God's work

> "As the Father has sent me, I am sending you."
>
> John 20:21
>
>
>
> "He who believes in Me, the works that I do, he will do also; and greater works than these ... because I go to the Father."
>
> John 14:12, NASB

Mission impossible: "Daddy, hep"

answered prayers
Help us for the
glory of God.
It reminds us
it's God's power.

Theme 2: prayer to God's glory

Help us, O God our Savior, for the *glory* of your name.

Psalm 79:9

———————————————— ◎ ————————————————

"I will do whatever you ask in my name, so that the Son may bring *glory* to the Father."

John 14:13

John Piper says in *Let the Nations Be Glad* that God's chief end is to glorify himself. He will bring himself glory by entering into the warfare and becoming the main combatant.

VIDEO DISCUSSION #1

1. Looking back at the Bible passage and your video teaching notes, what did you learn that you did not know previously? Consider specifically:

   • The number of times Jesus promises to answer our prayers

   • The importance of doing God's work/<u>mission</u>

   • The need to pray for help

   • The importance of praying for God's glory and his work

   How does this knowledge help you to understand Jesus' promise better?

2. If we are supposed to pray for help in accomplishing God's work in the world and for his glory, do you think that this means that we can never pray for our own needs? Why or why not?

3. What "work of God" are you asking Jesus to help you accomplish?

GOING DEEPER

"In Jesus' name" means that we are acting as his representatives.

Video Teaching #2 Notes

Theme 3: praying "in Jesus' name"

Greek background: "in the name of"

In his name
Demons macced do
magic for you.
Homer's Iliad.
calling on any
deity to help me.

SAMPLE GREEK PRAYERS

God with the silver bow, protector of Chryse, sacred Cilla,
mighty lord of Tenedos, Sminthean Apollo,
hear my prayer: If I've ever pleased you
with a holy shrine, or burned bones for you —
bulls and goats well wrapped in fat —
grant me my prayer. Force the Danaans
to pay full price for my tears with your arrows.

Homer's *Iliad* 1.38

I conjure you up, holy beings and holy names; join in aiding this spell
and ... destroy, kill, break Eucherius the charioteer, and all his horses
tomorrow in the circus at Rome.

With the proper formula, a spirit-induced sickness could be cured, a
chariot race could be won, and sexual passions could be enhanced.

Clint Arnold

Are prayers in Jesus' name magic?

"Whatever you ask" does not mean whatever might be on your wish list.

Andrew Lincoln

> Some Jews ... went around driving out evil spirits.... They would say, "In the name of Jesus, whom Paul preaches, I command you to come out." ... One day the evil spirit answered them, "Jesus I know, and I know about Paul, but who are you?" Then the man who had the evil spirit jumped on them and overpowered them all.
>
> Acts 19:13–16

What does the phrase "in Jesus' name" mean?

Remain in Jesus

abide.
Stay joined
stayed tied to Jesus.

> "If you remain in me and my words remain in you, ask whatever you wish, and it will be given you."
>
> John 15:7

Will we seek, through loyal obedience and love, to deepen our unity with the Father and the Son, and so become "friends" of God? As we do we will learn to allow our asking to be shaped by God's will and purposes, and so shall God be glorified in the answers.

M. M. B. Turner

Loving and obeying Jesus

> "As the Father has loved me, so have I loved you. Now remain in my love. If you obey my commands, you will remain in my love, just as I have obeyed my Father's commands and remain in his love."
>
> John 15:9–10

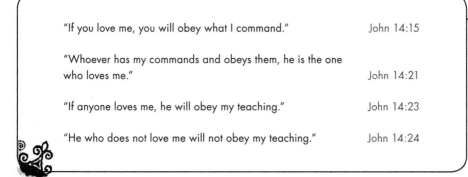

"If you love me, you will obey what I command." John 14:15

"Whoever has my commands and obeys them, he is the one who loves me." John 14:21

"If anyone loves me, he will obey my teaching." John 14:23

"He who does not love me will not obey my teaching." John 14:24

Assurance of answered prayer

This is the confidence we have in approaching God: that if we ask anything according to his will, he hears us. And if we know that he hears us — whatever we ask — we know that we have what we asked of him.

1 John 5:14–15

This is not intended to rationalize unanswered prayer but to encourage prayer that is in line with the will of God, as revealed in Christ.

Andrew Lincoln

Acting as Jesus' representatives in prayer

> As I read and meditate on the Word morning by morning, I try to allow it to shape my prayers ... by my saying to God things I would not have said had I not just previously been filling my mind and heart with his Word.
>
> Felicity Houghton

Power of attorney

"Prayer checks:" signing Jesus' name

> Praying "if it is your will" does not demonstrate a lack of faith, but a lack of knowledge of God's will in a specific situation.
>
> Terrance Tiessen

VIDEO DISCUSSION #2

1. Just as Matt Williams's brother signed $1 dividend checks and deposited them in his own account, what liberties have you taken in your prayer life when you have prayed for things that do not line up with the character and desires of Jesus? How can we be sure that we are praying for things that line up with Jesus' character?

2. Do you think that it is necessary to end every prayer with the phrase "in Jesus' name?" Why or why not?

3. Give examples of the kinds of prayer that you think God would answer based on these three themes—doing God's work, to his glory, and in Jesus' name.

CONNECTING THE BIBLE TO LIFE

If we pray for help to continue his work, to his glory, in the name of Jesus, our prayer lives will be revolutionized.

Video Teaching #3 Notes

The kind of prayer God answers

First, do our prayers seek God's help to further his work?

We are working with God to determine the future! We are to change the world through prayer.

Richard Foster

Prayer has bridled the rage of lions, extinguished wars, appeased the elements, expelled demons, burst the chains of death, and stayed the sun in its course.

Chrysostom, early church father

Second, do our prayers seek God's glory?

He is not going to help us develop our own kingdoms when we are called to establish his kingdom!

Neil Anderson

Third, do we pray "in the name of Jesus"?

love &
obey
listen

Is WWJD
W Jesus PrT that
asked

> What is necessary is an increasing knowledge of the Scriptures so that we may learn how to pray with confidence in Jesus' name.
>
> D. A. Carson

WJPT

> Brother Yun, one of China's house church leaders, prayed and fasted for months before receiving a Bible in 1974. When he received it he said, "Every day from morning to late evening I read the Word of God.... I finished reading through the whole Bible, so I started to memorize one chapter per day. After twenty-eight days I had memorized the whole gospel of Matthew."
>
> Paul Hattaway

Guaranteed answers?

"My Father, if it is possible, may this cup be taken from me. Yet not as I will, but as you will."

Matthew 26:39 (see also v. 42)

"O Jerusalem, Jerusalem, you who kill the prophets and stone those sent to you, how often I have longed to gather your children together, as a hen gathers her chicks under her wings, but you were not willing."

Matthew 23:37

"May they be brought to complete unity to let the world know that you sent me."

John 17:23

This is our comfort, because God answers every prayer; for either he gives what we pray for, or something far better.

Søren Kierkegaard

Lung cancer: God answers prayers

As a parent gives to a child from his or her wisdom what the child needs, so does God. Consequently, we may receive answers we do not want, find things we are not looking for, and have doors open we do not expect.

David Garland

VIDEO DISCUSSION #3

1. Can you relate to what Matt Williams said about his prayer for his dad? Have you prayed for something that you thought was in the will of God only to receive something different? Do you think God's answer was something better? Explain.

2. Matt Williams said that answered prayer comes about as we pray "in Jesus' name," which means that we must love and obey Jesus in every area of our lives. Prayer is not just a time that we set aside from our schedule to pray. Rather, our whole life affects our prayer life, and vice versa. How would your life be different if you lived out this truth?

3. How would your prayer life be different if you began to pray with these three themes in mind: Jesus' name, to God's glory, and for his work in the world? About what sorts of things would you spend more time praying than you do now? Take some time right now to pray for these things.

MAKING DEEPER CONNECTIONS IN YOUR OWN LIFE

Personal reflection studies to do on your own

Day One

1. Read John 15:1–11.

2. Do you normally think about God's glory when you pray? Why or why not? How would your prayer life be different if you did think about God's glory in your prayers?

3. Do you normally seek God's help in accomplishing the work/mission which he has given you to do in this world? What do you think would happen if you asked for his help more regularly?

4. We are all given at least one "work" of God to do in our lives: whether it is raising our family, being a light in the business world, doing our very best in school, or starting an inner-city mission. Write down what might be your primary "work" for God, then determine how much of it you do on your own versus how much of it you bathe in prayer.

Day Two

1. Read John 15:12–17.

2. The Greeks prayed in the names of their gods and demons hoping to influence them to do what they wanted. They assumed that their gods were cruel, fickle, and easily offended. Our God, however, is good, loving, and desirous of giving his children good gifts (see Matthew 7:11). How does it impact your prayers knowing that you have a good Father who wants to answer them?

3. The Greeks thought that they could coerce the gods into doing what they desired. If our God is sovereign, why do you think that he has asked us to pray to him? Do you think that we can influence the outcome of events through our prayers? Why or why not?

Day Three

1. Read John 16:16–24.

2. What role do you think the Holy Spirit plays in your praying (see Romans 8:26–27)?

3. The Chinese house church movement has learned the importance of knowing Jesus and praying "in his name." David Wang wrote, "And then it was Sister Yang's turn [to pray]. In a most natural and free-flowing manner, she began to pray in the language of Scripture. Quoting passages from Romans to Genesis to Philippians to the Psalms, Sister Yang used Scripture throughout her entire prayer of ten to fifteen minutes." Recent surveys show, by contrast, that the American church is becoming more biblically illiterate. What difference would it make in our prayers if we knew more biblical content? What about you? Do your prayers contain Scripture?

Day Four

1. Read Matthew 26:36–46.

2. If it is true that our good God desires to answer our prayers, does this mean that we always get what we want? Why or why not? Try to think of specific biblical texts as you answer this question.

3. If Jesus did not always receive what he prayed for (see Matthew 23:37; 26:39; John 17:23), what does that tell us about the tendencies of some Christians to think that the reason we do not get what we pray for is due to our own lack of faith?

Day Five

1. Read John 14:13–14 one more time.

2. Pray through the entire passage, allowing the deeper meaning that you have discovered to lead you as you pray. Ask the Spirit to continue to remind you of what you have learned and to help you apply these truths to your life.

3. Turn back to the discussion questions from the video teaching (Video Discussion #1, #2, #3). If there are questions that your group did not have time to discuss or questions that you might like to think more about, use this time to review and reflect further.

Source Acknowledgments

(These are noted in order of appearance for each session. When quoted from a commentary, full source information can be found in "Books for Further Reading" beginning on page 123.)

Session 1

Page 11: Cullmann, *Prayer*, 17.
Page 16: Lane, *Mark*, 335.
Page 18: Witherington III, *Mark*, 378.
Page 20: Fackler, *Mark*, 422.
Page 22: Lane, *Mark*, 335.

Session 2

Page 29: Garland, *Mark*, 449.
Page 33: Morris, *Luke*, 287.
Page 36: Green, *Luke*, 641.
Page 37: Keener, *Bible Background Commentary*, 238.
Page 38: Marshall (in Longenecker), *Into God's Presence*, 131.
Page 40: Garland, *Mark*, 448.

Session 3

Page 47: Wright (in Longenecker), *Into God's Presence*, 132.
Page 51: Cullmann, *Prayer*, 47.
Page 51: Karris, *Prayer*, 19.
Page 55: Marshall (in Longenecker), *Into God's Presence*, 127.
Page 57: Carson, *Matthew, Mark, Luke*, 171.
Page 58: Keener, *Bible Background Commentary*, 62.

Session 4

Page 69: Marshall (in Longenecker), *Into God's Presence*, 131.
Page 72: Keener, *Bible Background Commentary*, 219.

Page 72: Turner (in Carson), *Teach Us to Pray*, 67.
Page 73: Nolland, *Luke*, 626.
Page 75: Bailey, *Poet and Peasant*, 133.
Page 76: Morris, *Luke*, 214.
Page 78: Ibid.

Session 5

Page 83: Card, *The Parable of Joy*, 201.
Page 86: Köstenberger, *Bible Backgrounds Commentary*, 152.
Page 89: Barton, *John*, 341.
Page 89: Longenecker, *Into God's Presence*, 164.
Page 90: Köstenberger, *Bible Backgrounds Commentary*, 154.
Page 92: Beasley-Murray, *John*, 306.
Page 93: Morris, *John*, 636.

Session 6

Page 99: Neil T. Anderson, *Praying by the Power of the Spirit* (Eugene, Ore.: Harvest House, 2003), 7.
Page 106: Clinton Arnold, *Ephesians, Power and Magic: The Concept of Power in Ephesians in Light of Its Historical Setting* (Grand Rapids, Mich.: Baker, 1992), 18.
Page 107: Lincoln (in Longenecker), *Into God's Presence*, 176.
Page 108: Turner (in Carson), *Teach Us to Pray*, 82–83.
Page 109: Lincoln (in Longenecker), *Into God's Presence*, 176.
Page 110: Houghton (in Carson), *Teach Us to Pray*, 306.
Page 110: Tiessen, *Providence and Prayer*, 339.
Page 112: Richard Foster, *Celebration of Discipline: The Path to Spiritual Growth* (San Francisco: Harper and Row, 1988), 35.
Page 112: Anderson, *Praying by the Power of the Spirit*, 17.
Page 113: Carson, *Farewell Discourse and Final Prayer of Jesus*, 110.
Page 113: Paul Hattaway, *The Heavenly Man: The Remarkable True Story of Chinese Christian Brother Yun* (Grand Rapids, Mich.: Monarch Books, 2002), 26–33.
Page 114: Garland, *Mark*, 449.

Map and Photo Credits

Books for Further Reading

Four Gospels

Evans, Craig A., gen. ed. *The Bible Knowledge Background Commentary: Matthew–Luke.* Colorado Springs: Victor Books, 2003.

Keener, Craig S. *The IVP Bible Background Commentary: New Testament.* Downers Grove, Ill.: InterVarsity Press, 1993.

Matthew

Barton, Bruce B. *Matthew.* Life Application Bible Commentary. Wheaton, Ill.: Tyndale, 1996.

Blomberg, Craig L. *Matthew.* New American Commentary, vol. 22. Nashville: Broadman Press, 1992.

Carson, D. A. *Matthew, Mark, Luke.* The Expositor's Bible Commentary, vol. 8. Grand Rapids, Mich.: Zondervan, 1984.

———. *When Jesus Confronts the World: An Exposition of Matthew 8–10.* Grand Rapids, Mich.: Baker, 1987.

Davies, W. D. and Dale C. Allison, Jr. *A Critical and Exegetical Commentary on the Gospel According to Saint Matthew.* The International Critical Commentary. 3 vols. Edinburgh: T. & T. Clark, 1988, 1991, 1997.

France, R. T. *The Gospel According to Matthew: An Introduction and Commentary.* Tyndale New Testament Commentaries, vol. 1. Grand Rapids, Mich.: Eerdmans, 1985.

Green, Michael. *The Message of Matthew: The Kingdom of Heaven.* The Bible Speaks Today Series. Downers Grove, Ill.: InterVarsity Press, 2000.

Guelich, Robert A. *Sermon on the Mount: A Foundation for Understanding.* Waco, Tex.: Word, 1982.

Gundry, Robert. *Matthew: A Commentary on His Handbook for a Mixed Church Under Persecution.* Grand Rapids, Mich.: Eerdmans, 2nd ed. 1994.

Hagner, Donald. *Matthew.* Word Biblical Commentary, vol. 33 a&b. Waco, Tex.: Word, 1993, 1995.

Keener, Craig S. *A Commentary on the Gospel of Matthew.* Grand Rapids, Mich.: Eerdmans, 1999.

Morris, Leon. *The Gospel According to Matthew.* The Pillar New Testament Commentary. Grand Rapids, Mich.: Eerdmans, 1992.

Mounce, Robert H. *Matthew.* New International Biblical Commentary, vol. 1. Peabody, Mass.: Hendrickson, 1991.

Nolland, John. *The Gospel of Matthew: A Commentary on the Greek Text.* The New International Greek Testament Commentary. Grand Rapids, Mich.: Eerdmans, 2005.

Simonetti, Manlio, ed. *Matthew: Ancient Christian Commentary on Scripture.* 2 vols. Downers Grove, Ill.: InterVarsity Press, 2002.

Turner, David and Darrell L. Bock. *Matthew/Mark.* Cornerstone Biblical Commentary. Wheaton, Ill.: Tyndale, 2006.

Wilkins, Michael J. *Matthew.* The NIV Application Commentary. Grand Rapids, Mich.: Zondervan, 2004.

———. *Zondervan Illustrated Bible Backgrounds Commentary,* vol. 1. Grand Rapids, Mich.: Zondervan, 2002.

Mark

Cole, R. Alan. *The Gospel According to Mark.* Tyndale New Testament Commentaries, vol. 2. Grand Rapids, Mich.: Eerdmans, 2002.

Cranfield, C. E. B. *The Gospel According to Saint Mark: An Introduction and Commentary.* Cambridge Greek Testament Commentary. Cambridge, England: Cambridge University Press, 1972.

Edwards, James R. *The Gospel According to Mark.* The Pillar New Testament Commentary. Grand Rapids, Mich.: Eerdmans, 2002.

Evans, Craig. *Mark.* Word Biblical Commentary, vol. 34b. Nashville: Thomas Nelson, 2001.

Fackler, Mark. *Mark.* Life Application Bible Commentary. Wheaton, Ill.: Tyndale, 1994.

France, R. T. *The Gospel of Mark: A Commentary on the Greek Text.* The New International Greek New Testament Commentary. Grand Rapids, Mich.: Eerdmans, 2002.

Garland, David E. *Mark.* The NIV Application Commentary. Grand Rapids, Mich.: Zondervan, 1996.

———. *Zondervan Illustrated Bible Backgrounds Commentary,* vol. 1. Grand Rapids, Mich.: Zondervan, 2002.

Guelich, Robert A. *Mark.* Word Biblical Commentary, vol. 34a. Dallas: Word, 1989.

Gundry, Robert H. *Mark: A Commentary on His Apology for the Cross.* Grand Rapids, Mich.: Eerdmans, 1993.

Lane, William L. *The Gospel According to Mark: The English Text with Introduction, Exposition, and Notes.* The New International Commentary on the New Testament. Grand Rapids, Mich.: Eerdmans, 1974.

Mann, C. S. *Mark: A New Translation with Introduction and Commentary.* Garden City, N.Y.: Doubleday, 1986.

Oden, Thomas C. and Christopher A. Hall, eds. *Mark.* Ancient Christian Commentary on Scripture, vol. 2. Downers Grove, Ill.: InterVarsity Press, 1998.

Taylor, Vincent. *The Gospel According to St. Mark: The Greek Text with Introduction, Notes, and Indexes.* Thornapple Commentaries. Grand Rapids, Mich.: Baker, 2nd ed. 1981.

Wessel, Walter W. *Matthew, Mark, Luke.* The Expositor's Bible Commentary, vol. 8. Grand Rapids, Mich.: Zondervan, 1984.

Witherington, Ben III. *The Gospel of Mark: A Socio-Rhetorical Commentary.* Grand Rapids, Mich.: Eerdmans, 2001.

Luke

Barton, Bruce B., Dave Veerman, and Linda K. Taylor. *Luke.* Life Application Bible Commentary. Wheaton, Ill.: Tyndale, 1997.

Bock, Darrell L. *Luke.* The NIV Application Commentary. Grand Rapids, Mich.: Zondervan, 1996.

Evans, Craig A. *Luke.* New International Biblical Commentary, vol. 3. Peabody, Mass.: Hendrickson, 1990.

Fitzmyer, J. A. *The Gospel According to Luke: Introduction, Translation, and Notes.* Anchor Bible, vol. 28–28a. Garden City, N.Y.: Doubleday, 1981–1985.

Green, Joel B. *The Gospel of Luke.* New International Commentary on the New Testament. Grand Rapids, Mich.: Eerdmans, 1997.

Just, Arther A. Jr., ed. *Luke.* Ancient Christian Commentary on Scripture, vol. 3. Downers Grove, Ill.: InterVarsity Press, 2003.

Liefeld, Walter L. *Matthew, Mark, Luke.* The Expositor's Bible Commentary, vol. 8. Grand Rapids, Mich.: Zondervan, 1984.

Marshall, I. Howard. *Luke: Historian and Theologian.* Grand Rapids, Mich.: Zondervan, 1980.

Morris, Leon. *Luke: An Introduction and Commentary.* Tyndale New Testament Commentaries, vol. 3. Grand Rapids, Mich.: Eerdmans, 1988.

Nolland, John. *Luke.* Word Biblical Commentary, vol. 35a–c. Dallas: Word, 1989–1993.

Stein, Robert H. *Luke.* The New American Commentary, vol. 24. Nashville: Broadman Press, 1992.

Strauss, Mark L. *Zondervan Illustrated Bible Backgrounds Commentary,* vol. 1. Grand Rapids, Mich.: Zondervan, 2002.

John

Barrett, C. K. *The Gospel According to St. John: An Introduction with Commentary and Notes on the Greek Text.* Philadelphia: Westminster Press, 1978.

Barton, Bruce B. *John.* Life Application Bible Commentary. Wheaton, Ill.: Tyndale, 1993.

Beasley-Murray, George R. *John.* Word Biblical Commentaries, vol. 36. Nashville: Thomas Nelson, 1999.

Brown, Raymond Edward. *The Gospel According to John.* Anchor Bible, vol. 29–29a. Garden City, N.Y.: Doubleday, 1966–1970.

Burge, Gary M. *John.* The NIV Application Commentary. Grand Rapids, Mich.: Zondervan, 2000.

Card, Michael. *The Parable of Joy: Reflections on the Wisdom of the Book of John.* Nashville: Thomas Nelson, 1995.

Carson, D. A. *The Gospel According to John.* The Pillar New Testament Commentary. Grand Rapids, Mich.: Eerdmans, 1991.

Keener, Craig S. *The Gospel of John: A Commentary.* 2 vols. Peabody, Mass.: Hendrickson, 2003.

Köstenberger, Andreas J. *John.* Baker Exegetical Commentary on the New Testament. Grand Rapids, Mich.: Baker, 2004.

———. *Zondervan Illustrated Bible Backgrounds Commentary*, vol. 2. Grand Rapids, Mich.: Zondervan, 2002.

Morris, Leon. *The Gospel According to John.* New International Commentary on the New Testament. Grand Rapids, Mich.: Eerdmans, 1995.

Tasker, R. V. G. *The Gospel According to St. John: An Introduction and Commentary.* Tyndale New Testament Commentaries. Grand Rapids, Mich.: Eerdmans, 1960.

Tenney, Merrill C. *John, Acts.* The Expositor's Bible Commentary, vol. 9. Grand Rapids, Mich.: Zondervan, 1984.

Whitacre, Rodney A. *John.* The IVP New Testament Commentary Series, vol. 4. Downers Grove, Ill.: InterVarsity Press, 1999.

Prayer

Bounds, E. M. *The Complete Works of E. M. Bounds on Prayer.* Grand Rapids, Mich.: Baker, 1990.

Carson, D. A. *Teach Us to Pray: Prayer in the Bible and the World.* Grand Rapids, Mich.: Baker, 1994.

Chester, Timothy. *The Message of Prayer: Approaching the Throne of Grace.* Downers Grove, Ill.: InterVarsity Press, 2003.

Cullmann, Oscar. *Prayer in the New Testament.* Minneapolis: Fortress, 1995.

Crump, David. *Knocking on Heaven's Door: A New Testament Theology of Petitionary Prayer.* Grand Rapids, Mich.: Baker, 2006.

Foster, Richard J. *Prayer: Finding the Heart's True Home.* San Francisco: HarperSanFrancisco, 1992.

Karris, Robert J. *Prayer and the New Testament.* New York: Crossroad, 2000.

Brother Lawrence. *The Practice of the Presence of God.* Westminster, Md.: The Newman Book Shop, 1945.

Longenecker, Richard N. *Into God's Presence: Prayer in the New Testament.* Grand Rapids, Mich.: Eerdmans, 2001.

McKnight, Scot. *Praying with the Church: Following Jesus Daily, Hourly, Today.* Brewster, Mass.: Paraclete Press, 2006.

Piper, John. *A Hunger for God: Desiring God through Fasting and Prayer.* Wheaton, Ill.: Crossway, 1997.

Sittser, Gerald Lawson. *When God Doesn't Answer Your Prayer.* Grand Rapids, Mich.: Zondervan, 2004.

Tiessen, Terrance. *Providence and Prayer: How Does God Work in the World?* Downers Grove, Ill.: InterVarsity Press, 2000.

Willard, Dallas. *Hearing God: Developing a Conversational Relationship with God.* Downers Grove, Ill.: InterVarsity Press, 1999.

Wright, N. T. *The Lord and His Prayer.* Grand Rapids, Mich.: Eerdmans, 1997.

Yancey, Philip. *Prayer: Does It Make Any Difference?* Grand Rapids, Mich.: Zondervan, 2006.

Deeper Connections Series

The Miracles of Jesus

Six In-depth Studies Connecting the Bible to Life

Matt Williams, General Editor

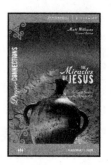

Healer of diseases. Master of nature. Conqueror of demons and death. Jesus not only preached the kingdom of God in word, but he demonstrated it in power through his miraculous deeds. This unique, in-depth look at the miracles of Jesus will open your eyes to their impact on the lives he touched, what they reveal about God's heart, and their significance for us today.

The 6 sessions are:
- The Clean Daughter (Mark 5:21–34)
- The Heartbeat of God (John 2:1–11)
- Knowing the King (Matt. 14:15–33)
- A Faith-full Outsider (Matt. 15:21–28)
- Fruitless Lives (Mark 11:12–21)
- Grateful Outcasts (Luke 17:11–19)

Taught and written by Bible professors, this unique DVD study with participant's guide explores the historical background of the Bible, its text, and its application for your life today. Filmed on location in the US and Israel, the Deeper Connections series is designed for small groups and Bible study classes.

DVD: 0-310-27193-2
Participant's Guide: 0-310-27194-0

Also available:

The Parables of Jesus

DVD: 0-310-27190-8
Participant's Guide: 0-310-27191-6